Make the Leap Coach's Guide

Questions and Activities to help your athletes get the most out of their training.

By Bryan Green

Make the Leap Coach's Guide: Questions and Activities to help your athletes get the most out of their training

Cover Artwork by Nadine Denten (@nadineinjapan)

makeheleapbook.com
maketheleapbook@gmail.com
@maketheleapbook

Coaches' Praise for *Make the Leap*

"If *Make the Leap* had been available I would have strongly encouraged the athletes I've coached over the years to read it at the start of each season. Furthermore I would have suggested that they review the book whenever they ran into mental or physical blocks."
- Bob Larsen, 4xNCAA Coach of the Year, UCLA, Retired; 2004 US Olympic Distance Coach; Head Toad

"Make the Leap is a pathway book. A mental running clinic in book form, it allows an individualized approach for each person that reads it. It is a book I will read over and over again."
- Ken Reeves, 2x National Coach of the Year, 11x CA State Cross Country Champion at Nordhoff High

"In *Make the Leap* Bryan Green focuses on the mental factor as the primary determinant of running success ("think better, train better"), creating his own terminology to show how our minds can work for and against us. The book is an excellent resource for both runners and coaches to study and employ in their efforts to maximize potential and is applicable to all areas of life: athletic, professional, and personal."
- Walt Lange, 2010 National Coach of the Year, 9x CA State Cross Country Champion at Jesuit High

"THIS book belongs on the bookshelf of every competitive athlete and coach...not just running/track and field. It's the thinking man's guide to tapping into one's potential."
- Mike Fanelli, USA National Team Coach, 1992, 1996, 2000

"As Bryan Green points out in such engaging fashion, there is so much more to becoming a faster runner than logging miles. *Make the Leap* is a must-read book for athletes and coaches everywhere, a literal how-to of goals, attitude, and mindset to make better runners."
- Martin Dugard, 3x CA State Cross Country Champion, New York Times #1 bestselling author

"*Make the Leap* will transform how you think about your training, which in turn will transform your entire running experience. If you feel you have untapped potential, read this book."
- Matt Fitzgerald, 80/20 Endurance coach, Author of *80/20 Running* and *Chasing the Dream*

"The next leap forward in achieving higher levels of peak performance will come from understanding our mental relationship with running. *Make the Leap* provides an easy to use framework for improving your mental skills, honing a growth mindset, and achieving your potential."
- Jason Fitzgerald, Strength Running head coach and host of the Strength Running Podcast

"*Make the Leap* is a *legal* performance-enhancing aid for athletes and coaches alike. When you read this book, make sure you do so with a highlighter and pen in hand because there are non-stop "a-ha" moments. A "must-have" resource for the bookshelves of all endurance athletes and coaches."
- Scott Abbott, Director, Sacramento Running Association; former coach at Sacramento State University

"*Make the Leap* is the perfect complement to the many books on how to train to be a better runner, explaining how to think about your running and your life to create momentum that leads to breakthroughs."
- Jonathan Beverly, Editor-in-Chief at Podium Runner, Author of *Run Strong, Stay Hungry & Your Best Stride*

See more at maketheleapbook.com/praise

Hi Coach,

First off, thank you for all the time and effort you put into what you do. My coaches had a profound impact on my life, and it's my sincere hope that Make the Leap, the Think Better Workbook, and this Coaches' Guide help you get the most out of your athletes.

I wrote Make the Leap with your athletes in mind. I wanted to create a tool for young, competitive athletes to understand training in a broader, more productive way. The purpose of this Coaches' Guide is to help you give your athletes simple strategic opportunities to implement these ideas into their training. (*I should note: this guide assumes that both you and your athletes have read the book and have access to the workbook. If they don't, you may need to do a little more explaining.*)

One of the Optimal Training Principles I propose in Make the Leap is that engagement in training makes the process more understandable, more relevant, and more effective. Reading this book with your team–whether it's the whole text or a few targeted chapters–is a fantastic way to have your athletes engage with an aspect of their training that they may not have given much thought to: **how they think.**

By doing it as a team, you have the opportunity to embrace these frameworks, attitudes, and priorities together, and to give your team tools to reinforce those qualities on a daily basis. Sometimes all you need is a picture or a way to talk about an idea for it to become something athletes can relate to. Make the Leap will give you numerous options to choose from, and where you already have a framework you love, I'm confident the ideas in Make the Leap will enhance it.

This coaches' guide mirrors the chapters in Make the Leap. I include a short summary, my key takeaways from the end of each chapter, the main diagrams, a few summary questions to check understanding of the major themes, and some more provocative questions to stimulate thought and debate. I also include a Team Activity worksheet that you can do with your team to spark discussion and new ideas. These are particularly useful in a training camp or as a mid-season activity to get your athletes thinking better about a key area of training.

While Make the Leap is centered on running, your athletes can **apply the ideas in all areas of their lives**. They've not only helped me make a leap in training, they've helped me get better grades, learn languages, and excel in professional settings. They work wherever disciplined, focused effort is critical to achieving results.

Again, thank you for investing in your athletes and if you have any questions or feedback for me, please connect with me. I'd love to learn from you.

Go Be More,

Bryan Green
bryan@maketheleapbook.com

The Optimal Training Principles

1. Your athletic performance is a result of your attitude, your effort, and your training methods.

2. Active engagement in training makes the process more understandable, more relevant, and more effective. (And more fun.)

3. You are responsible for your own training.

4. Ability is a variable, not a constant. The harder you work, the more able you become.

5. Self-efficacy is a fundamental ingredient to overcoming obstacles and achieving success.

6. All behavior is caused. All causation is mental. We become what we think about most of the time.

7. Optimal training is centered on clear, executable goals. We train to improve specific abilities.

8. Certain behaviors, if practiced with consistent quality, ensure Optimal Training.

9. Making mistakes is an effective way to learn and improve.

10. Racing times and personal records indicate progress at one point in time.

11. Optimal performances and realizing your potential are results of painstaking preparation and hard work.

The Four Spotlights

1. The Momentum Model - a simple tool to understand what's driving you forward, and what's holding you back

2. Attribution Theory - what we say defines how we think; and high achievers speak differently from low achievers

3. The 80/20 Rule - not all behaviors drive the same results; when we identify what really matters we get much more out of our time and effort

4. Next Level 80/20 - when we get serious about applying the 80/20 rule, we see that most of our progress comes from just a few activities

Chapter 1 Summary Questions

Feedback loops: Feedback Loops have 4 parts: input, process, output, feedback. Input and output are *us*, before and after the workout. Feedback is the change we retain, and can be positive or negative. The goal is to produce–and retain–a small improvement with each workout. *We want athletes to look at training as being more than just the "training" box and emphasize the recovery/feedback portion as well.*
- Training is the process. What are some examples of "training activities"? Why do we do them?
- Feedback is our recovery. What are some examples of "recovery activities"? Why do we do them?
- What are some examples of activities that disrupt your feedback loop?
- How many times do you think you need to repeat your feedback loop in order to truly see the benefits?

Leap Cycles: Experiencing a "leap" is normal in learning and effort-based skills and abilities. Often when we struggle to do something and then it "clicks" we've made a small leap. It typically follows 3 phases: we work hard but see little improvement (Build), then it clicks (Leap), and then we settle into a new normal (Sustain). *We want athletes to appreciate that not seeing results today is not indicative of a lack of improvement and that the better the overall feedback loop, the bigger/sooner the potential leap.*
- What are the characteristics of the Build phase? How long does it take to reach the Leap phase?
- What are the characteristics of the Leap phase? How long does it last?
- What are the characteristics of the Sustain phase? How long does it take to reach another Build phase?
- How many leaps can you make in your life?

Thought-provoking questions to spark your athletes' interest/imagination.
- Why do so many athletes make the leap after a summer vacation?
- What benefits do track middle distance runners get out of doing cross country?
- Feedback loops are dependent on quality, recovery, and consistency. Which is the most important?
- What is the weakest part of your personal feedback loop?
- Which ideas seem applicable to other areas of your life?
- Which workout is more important: today's, tomorrow's, or the one in four days?
- What 3 words would you choose to define a strong training feedback loop? *(Bryan's choice: quality, recovery, consistency)*

Key Takeaways

1. Anyone can make a leap in their performance. A leap is the natural output of maintaining a positive feedback loop in your training.

2. Improvement appears linear in the beginning but is actually exponential. Consistent, high quality training leads to making a leap.

3. A "leap cycle" has three main stages–Build, Leap, and Sustain–and can be repeated indefinitely until you reach your potential.

4. All leaps are preceded by a change in training quality. If your quality doesn't improve after making a leap, you will not make another one.

Feedback Loop

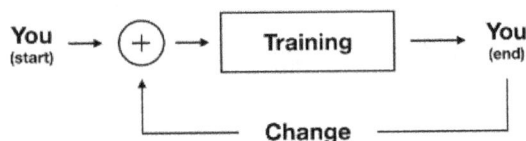

Leap Cycle

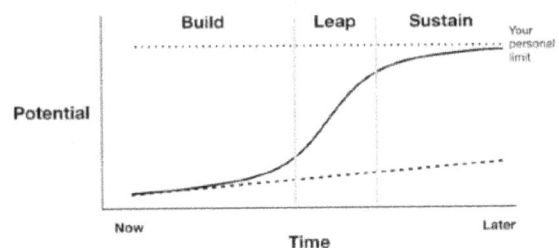

Team Activity - Feedback Loops

Imagine a typical day of training. What training activities do you do? What recovery activities? In the white boxes, write as many training and recovery activities as you can. Then compare to the answers your teammates came up with.

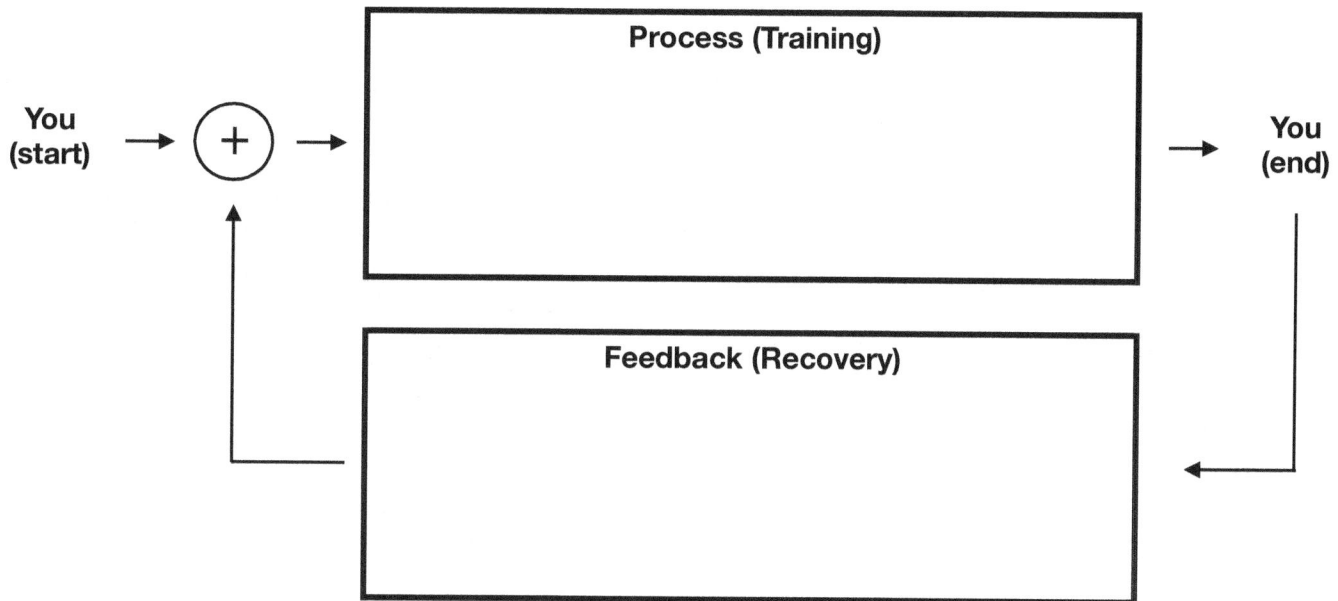

You (start) → (+) → | **Process (Training)** | → **You (end)**

| **Feedback (Recovery)** |

Takeaways

Write down any observations, strategies, or personal goals you want to make sure you remember.

"I think it's very important to have a feedback loop, where you're constantly thinking about what you've done and how you could be doing it better." - Elon Musk

Momentum Model Summary Questions

The Momentum Model is a simple diagram that helps us to talk about both the key forces and factors affecting our performance, as well as the effect they have on our progress. Internal and external forces can be positive or negative, strong or weak. They drive us up a hill, whose height corresponds to how difficult our goal is. As we ascend the hill we also need to prepare for and overcome obstacles that will slow us down. *We want athletes to be able to articulate and express the positive and negative factors driving their success in a way that allows them to compare them, contextualize them, and strategize for them.*

- What are some positive forces that drive you forward?
- What are some negative forces that hold you back?
- What are the three types of obstacles we typically encounter?
- How does the Momentum Model connect to the idea of feedback loops and making a leap?

5 Insights

1. The size of the arrow indicates its strength. Not all arrows are equally strong.

2. The size of an arrow changes over time. We can strategically strengthen and weaken the forces that drive our momentum.

3. The direction of an arrow is not fixed. A positive force today can turn negative tomorrow.

4. We can't perfectly measure all the arrows affecting us. It is sufficient to ask: is it positive or negative? And is it as strong or as weak as we'd like it to be?

5. Talent is best understood as the size of our ball. Talent is not an internal force. It is us. A talented person may have advantages, but those can often be overcome by effort and aligning your forces.

Thought-provoking questions to spark your athletes' interest/imagination.
- Can something be considered "good for us" but still be a negative force in our training?
- Have you ever turned a negative into a positive? What did you do?
- Some athletes struggle to train well when they go from high school to college. Others thrive. How can the Momentum Model explain this?
- Why do training camps have so many positive effects for most runners?
- When you *feel* successful, you tend to run better. Does this make sense in the Momentum Model?
- Should you choose a really crazy goal with a huge hill, or an easier to achieve goal with a more reasonable hill to climb? Why?
- What is the one force most athletes underestimate? Why do you think they underestimate it?

The Momentum Model

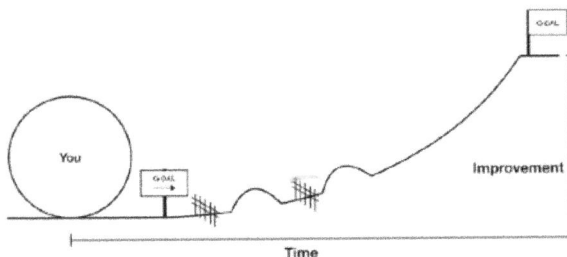

The Forces

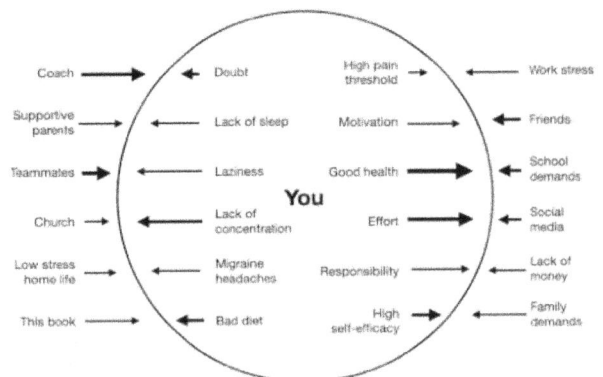

Team Activity - Momentum Model

Below is a section of your Momentum Model. Think about your goal. Write as many positive and negative forces as you can come up with. Then circle the 5 biggest forces. Compare to your teammates' answers.

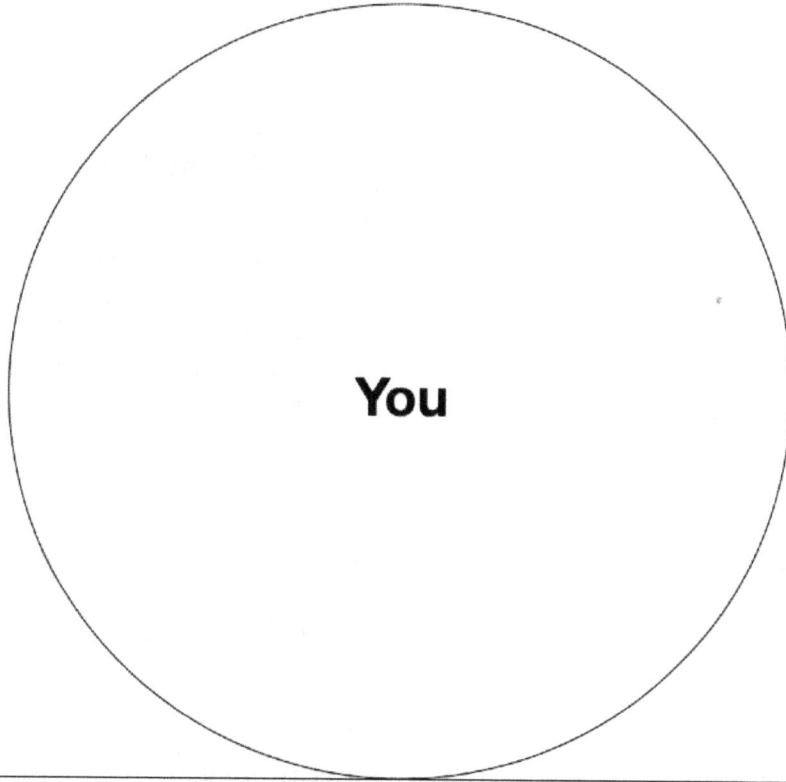

You

Takeaways

Write down any observations, strategies, or personal goals you want to make sure you remember.

"Success requires first expending ten units of effort to produce one unit of results.
Your momentum will then produce ten units of results with each unit of effort." - Charles J. Givens

Chapter 2 Summary Questions

Optimal Training Principle #1: Your athletic performance is a result of your attitude, your effort, and your training methods

I place attitude at the foundation of the Optimal Training Pyramid. Attitude is more than just motivation, passion or confidence. It includes how we view and understand the world, because that affects the expectations we set. Effort rests on top of it. The quality of our effort is best measured in efficiency and effectiveness. Finally our training methods sit at the very top. *We want athletes to appreciate that we often have areas where we can improve our attitude, and when they do it will unlock better effort and training.*

- What are some other words for "attitude"? What are some examples of good attitudes?
- What are some other words for "effort"? How do you measure effort?
- What are some other words for "training methods"? Why are training methods at the top and not the bottom of the pyramid?
- The author says it's better to get 100% out of a good workout than 70% out of a perfect workout. What is his argument?

Key Takeaways

1. Your attitude, effort, and training methods are the three driving forces for all performances. Of these, attitude is the most important, because it determines the quality of the other two.

2. Quality, quantity and time are all critical aspects of our training. For most athletes, quality and time are sufficient to make their first leap.

3. Your focus should be on maximum efficiency, because it creates positive feedback loops and helps to identify opportunities to improve your training effectiveness.

Thought-provoking questions to spark your athletes' interest/imagination.
- Two runners have equal physical talent. What is most likely to set them apart?
- Can you have a bad attitude but still have good effort?
- Does the phrase "coach the person, not the skill" relate to this idea?
- Are there specific attitudes that a team should try to build?
- Is attitude something we can change or is it fixed, something we just need to deal with?
- Two coaches have the same training programs. Will they get the same results from their teams?
- True or False: Until we've mastered the highest quality activities, we shouldn't worry about the rest.

Optimal Training Pyramid

Efficiency vs Effectiveness

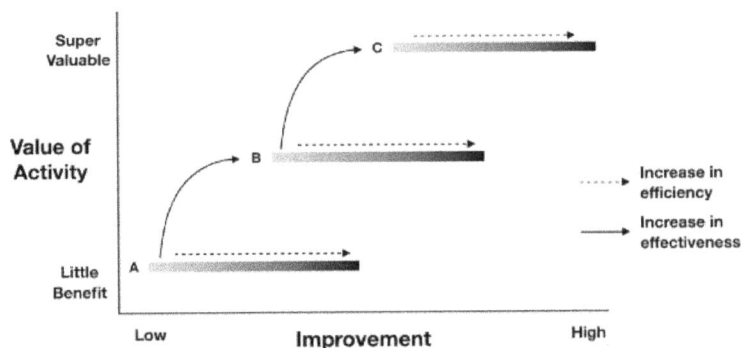

Team Activity - Optimal Training Pyramid

Below is an image of the Optimal Training Pyramid. In the space to the right, write as many examples or key ideas to keep in mind for each part. Then compare to the answers your teammates came up with.

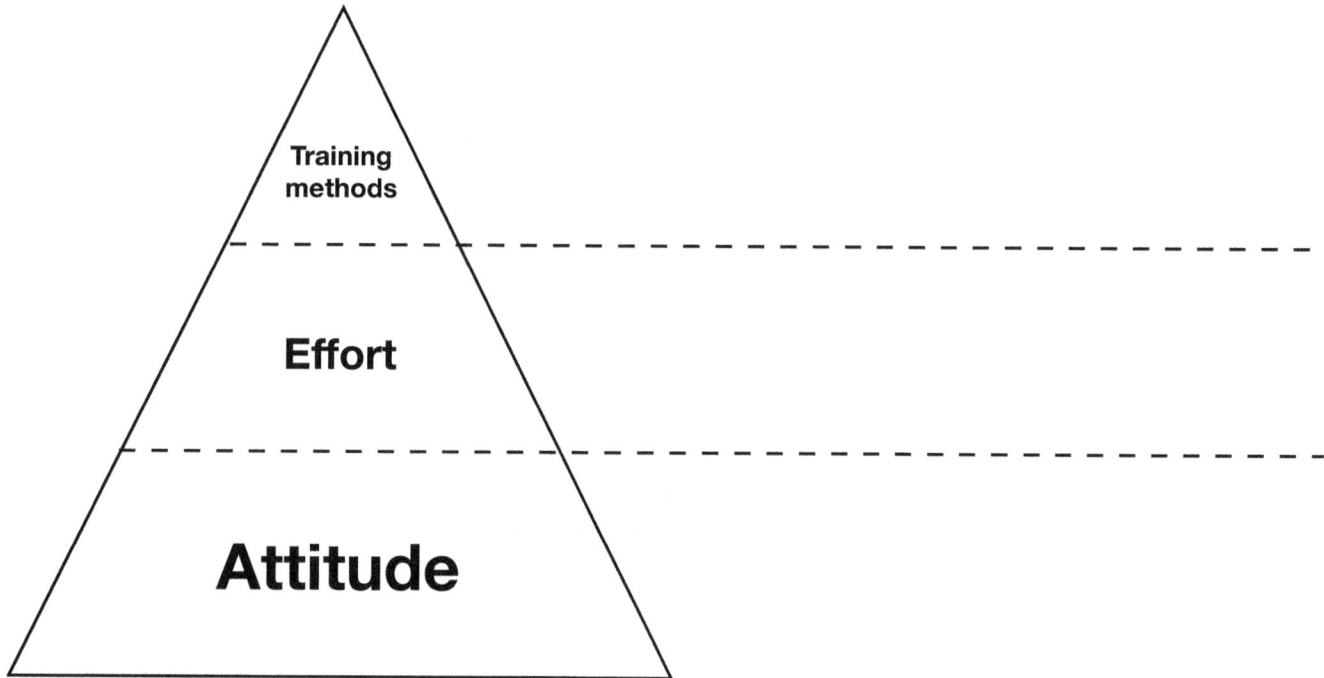

```
        /\
       /  \
      / Training \
     / methods \
    /- - - - - - - - - - - - - - - - - - - - - - - - -
   /            \
  /    Effort     \
 /                  \
/- - - - - - - - - - - - - - - - - - - - - - - - -
/                      \
/       Attitude          \
/_____\
```

Takeaways

Write down any observations, strategies, or personal goals you want to make sure you remember.

"Ability is what you're capable of doing. Motivation determines what you do.
Attitude determines how well you do it." - Lou Holtz

Chapter 3 Summary Questions

Optimal Training Principle #2: Active engagement in training makes the process more understandable, more relevant, and more effective. (And more fun.)

Engagement is one of the key attitudes that drive success. The quality of your engagement is the product of your motivation (desire to achieve a goal) and your passion (desire to do an activity). The more you engage in your craft, the more expertise you gain and the more likely you are to reveal the hidden training program: what **you** *really* need to do to be successful. Engagement is a skill that can be trained like any other. *We want athletes to realize that cultivating their motivation and passion for all aspects of training is key to success.*

- What does "engaging" in the sport mean to you?
- Why does increased engagement lead to improved performance?
- What are some examples of the Hidden Training Program?
- Is the hidden training program always hidden, or can we make it visible?

Thought-provoking questions to spark your athletes' interest/imagination.
- Is everybody's hidden training program the same? What is different?
- Who needs to engage more, athletes in team sports or individual sports?
- Can you share an example when you learned something new that made you a better athlete?
- What is the most important part of the hidden training program? Where should athletes focus first?
- Is there any connection between intelligence and engagement?
- What is the difference between being engaged, immersed, and obsessed?

Key Takeaways

1. Engagement is a key Optimal Training attitude. By engaging you improve your understanding, your perspective, and your effectiveness.

2. The Hidden Training Program is everything you "really" need to do to be successful. Engagement is the best way to reveal the hidden training program.

3. Increasing engagement doesn't require huge efforts. It is sufficient to start small by reading, talking, and asking about your training.

**Engagement =
Passion x Motivation**

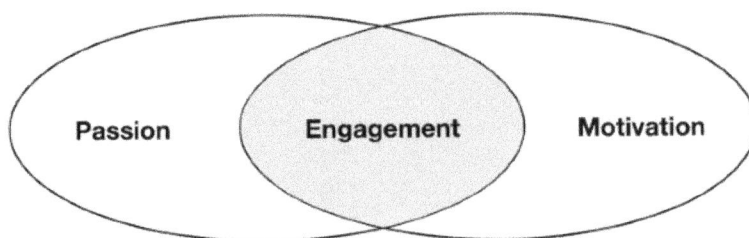

Hidden Training Program

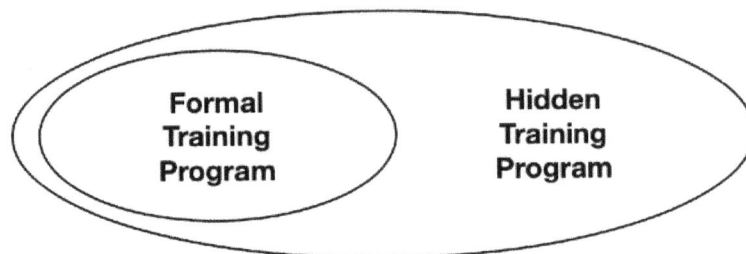

Team Activity - Hidden Training Program

Write down areas of the Hidden Training Program that are easy to overlook or under-appreciate. How many could be moved into the Formal Training Program? Compare to the answers your teammates came up with.

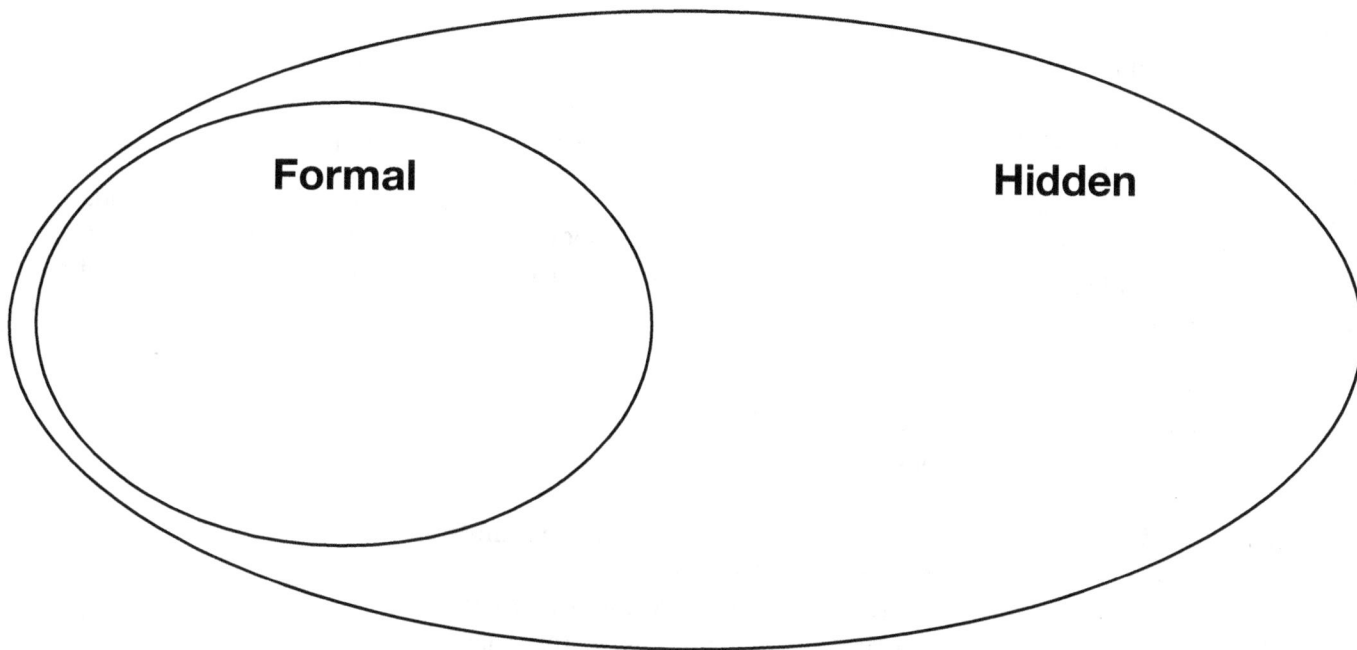

Formal

Hidden

Takeaways

Write down any observations, strategies, or personal goals you want to make sure you remember.

"To succeed, work hard, never give up, and above all cherish a magnificent obsession." - Walt Disney

Chapter 4 Summary Questions

Optimal Training Principle #3: You are responsible for your own training.

There are 3 key phases of training: planning, execution, and evaluation. Many athletes take responsibility for executing the workout and leave planning and evaluation to their coach. But the best athletes take responsibility for ALL aspects of their training, including their relationship with their coach. *We want athletes to accept that their results are their responsibility and that their relationship with the coach requires consideration as well.*

- What is an example of a "planning" activity?
- What is an example of an "execution" activity?
- What is an example of an "evaluation" activity?
- What does it mean to "get the most out of your coach"?

Thought provoking questions that may spark their interest/imagination.
- A race plan doesn't lead to a good result. Whose fault is it?
- What's the most important part of the athlete/coach relationship to get right?
- If athletes are responsible for their results, what are coaches responsible for?
- Are you responsible for things that are outside your control? If yes, in what way?
- How are engagement and responsibility connected to each other?
- You and your coach have a different evaluation of your performance? Who is right?

Key Takeaways

1. You are responsible for all aspects of your training, including planning, execution, and evaluation.

2. Your coach's role is to provide you the best possible guidance toward achieving your goals. You must engage with your coach to ensure you are getting the feedback you need.

3. Being responsible for the results means looking to yourself first when evaluating why you aren't performing to the level you aspire.

Optimal Division of Responsibility

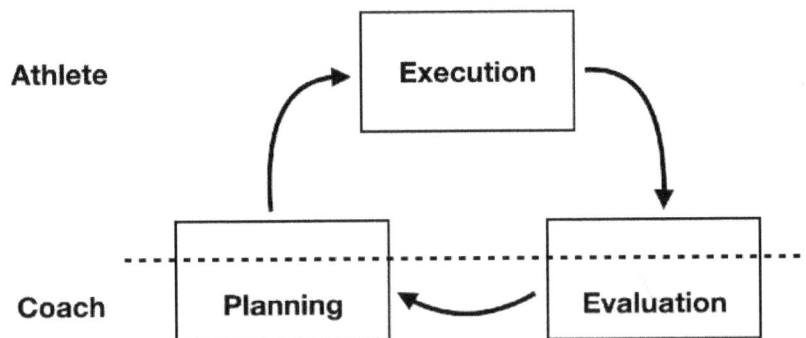

Responsibility for Hidden Training Program

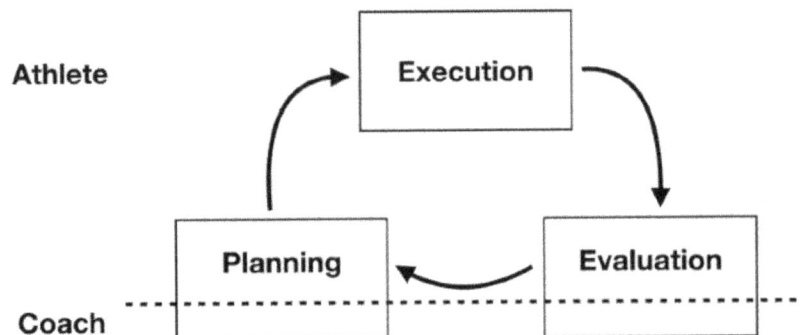

Team Activity - Responsibility

What are some ways you can participate in the Planning and Evaluation of your training? What roles should stay with your coach? Compare to the answers your teammates came up with.

Planning	Evaluation

Takeaways

Write down any observations, strategies, or personal goals you want to make sure you remember.

"The greatest day in your life and mine is when we take total responsibility for our attitudes. That's the day we truly grow up." - John C. Maxwell

Attribution Theory Summary Questions

Attribution theory looks at one of the central ways high achievers think differently from low achievers. It isolates the way we interpret and explain results, and what that means for how we think about performance. High achievers tend to explain results in ways that give them maximum benefit. Low achievers explain results in ways that lead them to give up. *We want athletes to develop a habit of attributing their results to controllable factors, and not to internalize failures as being associated with their talent.*

- What are the four main factors that all performance is attributed to?
- Which factors are stable? Which factors are internal? Which factors are controllable?
- What does "high achievers and low achievers tell different stories" mean to you?
- Green's Razor says, "Never attribute to talent or luck that which is adequately explained by effort." What is the benefit of following this rule?

5 Insights

1. High achievers internalize success. Low achievers externalize success.

2. High achievers view failure as variable. Low achievers view failure as fixed.

3. High achievers view results as controllable. Low achievers do not.

4. Attribution is a learned behavior. We learn it from copying those around us. We can learn to attribute better.

5. Attribution can become a habit. The more we consistently attribute like a high achiever, the better we set expectations and understand our results.

Thought-provoking questions to spark your athletes' interest/imagination.
- Which factor do you believe is most important for running? What about school? Art? Public speaking?
- Can you attribute to more than one factor at a time? Should you?
- Attribution theory assumes talent is fixed. Do you think that's true?
- Think about one of your biggest successes. What role did effort and preparation play in it?
- Think about one of your biggest failures. What role did effort and preparation play in it?
- Can you prepare in a way that makes the task difficulty easier?
- There is a saying, "Chance favors the prepared mind." Do you agree?

The Four Factors

Stability

Locus of Control		Fixed	Variable
Internal		Talent	Effort
External		Task Difficulty	Luck

Controllable

High Achievers vs Low Achievers

Attribution

Athlete		Success	Failure
High Achiever		• Talented • Worked hard	• Didn't work hard • Underestimated task • Bad luck
Low Achiever		• Task was easy • Lucky	• Not talented • Task too difficult

Team Activity - Attribution Theory

So much of what we say highlights how we think. What are some of the words you often use when you talk about the four factors. Compare to the answers your teammates came up with.

Talent	Effort
Task Difficulty	Luck

Takeaways

Write down any observations, strategies, or personal goals you want to make sure you remember.

"Work ethic is important because, unlike intelligence, athleticism, charisma, or any other natural attribute, it's a choice." - Mike Rowe

Chapter 5 Summary Questions

Optimal Training Principle #4: Ability is a variable, not a constant. The harder you work, the more able you become.

How we think about talent has a huge effect on how much effort we put into things. If we have a fixed mindset, we limit ourselves and focus on demonstrating our talent. If we have a growth mindset we strive to continuously improve. The way we set goals can also affect how we think about success and whether it is achievable. Norm-referenced goals are based on comparisons to standards or others. Self-referenced goals focus on context and process. The best performers are often equally driven by self-referenced goals. *We want athletes to consider their views on talent and aim to emphasize effort and process more.*

- What is the key characteristic of a Fixed Mindset? Can runners have a fixed mindset?
- What is the key characteristic of a Growth Mindset? Can runners have a growth mindset?
- What are norm-referenced goals?
- What are self-referenced goals?

Key Takeaways

1. Norm-referenced goals are measured against external factors. Self-referenced goals are measured against internal factors. Excellence is often measured against norm-referenced factors, but great athletes base their training on self-referenced factors.

2. People with a Fixed mindset believe that talent is something to be demonstrated, whereas those with a Growth mindset believe that ability is developed through effort.

3. A Fixed mindset can be developed into a Growth mindset through the Reframing Approach–emphasizing effort and preparation–and the Analogy Approach–finding an area that appears to be fixed and showing that it isn't.

Thought-provoking questions that may spark their interest/imagination.
- What kind of goals motivate you the most: norm-referenced or self-referenced?
- True or False: Faster runners have norm-referenced goals. Slower runners have self-referenced goals.
- Do you know someone with a Fixed mindset? Does it hold them back from being their best?
- Are there areas where *you* have a fixed mindset? Singing, art, math, languages? Do you believe you can be great at anything you put your mind to?
- Can you have a different mindset about different events? Do you have the same mindset about 200m as 5000m?
- Have you ever run a race where the only goal was to execute a plan, not get a final result? If so, how was it? If not, why might it be a good idea?

Norm vs Self-Referenced Performance

	Norm-Referenced	Self-Referenced
Short-term	Fast Time Winner of Race	Improvement Optimal Performance
Long-term	Champion All-Time List Hall of Fame	Fulfillment Realize Potential

Team Activity - Goal-Setting

Write down some of your short-term and long-term goals. Make sure you identify both norm-referenced and self-referenced goals. Compare to the answers your teammates came up with.

	Norm-Referenced Goals	Self-Referenced Goals
Short-term		
Long-term		

Takeaways

Write down any observations, strategies, or personal goals you want to make sure you remember.

"Over the course of time, if you work hard enough and you're dedicated enough at something, it's going to look like extreme talent." - Bryson DeChambeau

Chapter 6 Summary Questions

Optimal Training Principle #5: Self-efficacy is a fundamental ingredient to overcoming obstacles and achieving success.

Self-efficacy connects our growth mindset to the task at hand. The more self-efficacy we have, the more likely we are to persist and find a solution to our problems. Then, the act of persisting creates its own feedback loop in which we believe we are capable of persisting and doing more. The strongest way to increase self-efficacy is via personal experience, followed by seeing someone else you relate to accomplish a task. These are approaches that we can manufacture and/or seek out in training. *We want athletes to understand that efficacy changes with practice and that there are numerous strategies they can pursue to improve theirs.*

- What does self-efficacy mean to you?
- Why do personal experiences create the most self-efficacy?
- What is more valuable to you, vicarious experience (seeing someone else do it) or social persuasion (being told you can do it)?
- Do physiological factors (how your body feels), visualization, or faith have an effect on your self-efficacy?

Key Takeaways

1. Self-efficacy is the belief in what you can achieve based on the effort you put into a task.

2. You can improve your self-efficacy through various experiences. The most effective are personal experiences and vicarious experiences.

3. Persistence is pursuing a goal despite obstacles and difficulties, and changing tactics as necessary to achieve it. It is both a by-product and a contributor to self-efficacy.

Thought-provoking questions that may spark their interest/imagination.
- Two athletes have equal talent. Is there any reason for them to have different self-efficacy?
- Two people both tell you they believe in your ability. Is there any reason for one to boost your self-efficacy more than the other?
- Does more experience lead to higher self-efficacy?
- Do you get very nervous before races or tests? Does it affect how well you think you will do?
- Can you share a story where you got a big boost in self-efficacy?
- True or False: self-efficacy is a skill that you can improve with time. Why do you say that?
- Do clutch performers have higher self-efficacy?

The 4+2 Factors of Self-Efficacy

Type of Factor

Effect on Self-Efficacy	Internal	External
High	Personal Experience	Vicarious Experience
Low	Physiological; Visualization; Faith	Social Persuasion

Team Activity - Self-Efficacy

For each of the below areas, write down at least one way you can proactively create opportunities to boost your self-efficacy. Be as detailed as you can. Compare to the answers your teammates came up with.

Personal Experience (you did it or something like it)
Vicarious Experience (they did it, so you can, too)
Social Persuasion (someone says you can)
Other (physiological responses, visualization, faith)

Takeaways

Write down any observations, strategies, or personal goals you want to make sure you remember.

*"Self-belief does not necessarily ensure success,
but self-disbelief assuredly spawns failure." - Albert Bandura*

80/20 Rule Summary Questions

The 80/20 Rule is a useful reminder that our actions and our results are not proportional. Some behaviors are more effective than others. In fact, it's very common for the majority of our success (or failure) to be driven by a small number of causes. Activities that drive value should be prioritized and maximized, whereas activities that generate low value should be minimized and systematized. *We want athletes to think critically about their behaviors and put their energy into those activities that are most likely to generate the results they desire.*

- The 80/20 Rule says that our actions and our results are not proportional. What does that mean to you?
- We should maximize some activities and minimize others. How do we decide?
- What is "Negative 80/20"? Why is it important to understand in training?
- "Running is 90% mental. The other half is physical." Why does this make sense in the 80/20 Rule?

5 Insights

1. The 80/20 Rule is not a law of physics. It's a useful shortcut for making assumptions about the world.

2. The relationship is not always 80/20. The actual relationship could be any combination, and they don't need to add up to 100.

3. Not all areas of life can be explained by the 80/20 Rule. Some qualities, like talent or intelligence, are normally distributed in the population.

4. 80/20 thinking is a tool for prioritizing. Use it with scarce resources (time, energy) and a criteria for prioritizing them (profit, joy).

5. It can be easy to take it too far. If all the choices are too similar, then the 80/20 Rule doesn't help.

Thought-provoking questions to spark your athletes' interest/imagination.
- Which training activities fall in the 20%?
- What types of activities are in the "negative 20%", meaning they create the most friction?
- What is the 20% of your day that drives the majority of your success?
- What are some "rest of 80%" activities that we should do, but with minimal efforts?
- What are some 80/20 activities that drive success in school?
- Does the 80/20 rule apply to relationships? How so?
- Do you agree that running is, like baseball, 90% mental?

The 80/20 Rule

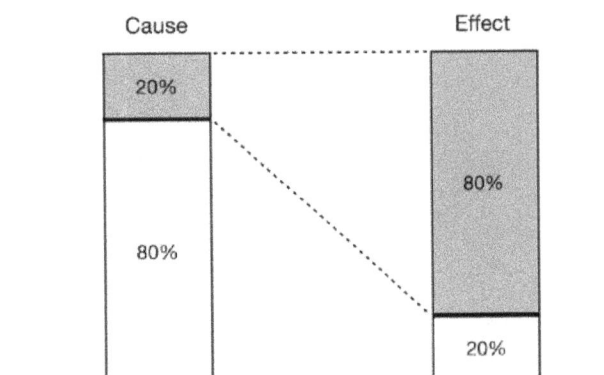

80/20 Forces

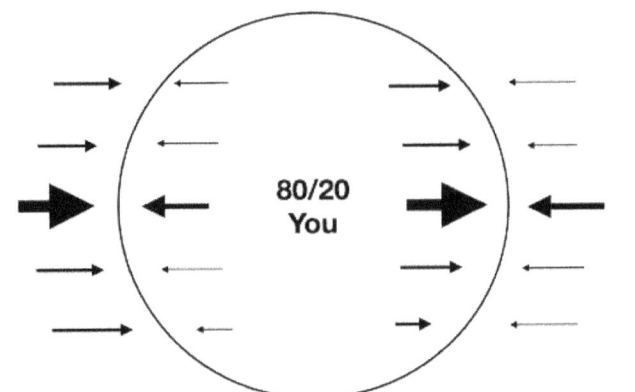

Team Activity - 80/20 Rule

Activities that generate big gains should be maximized. Activities that don't generate big gains should be minimized. Pick one Positive 80/20 and Negative 80/20 area and write an idea for how to improve it. Compare to the answers your teammates came up with.

	Positive 80/20	*Negative 80/20*
Maximize (top 20%)		
Minimize (rest-of 80%)		

Takeaways

Write down any observations, strategies, or personal goals you want to make sure you remember.

"It is not shortage of time that should worry us, but the tendency for the majority of time to be spent in low-quality ways." - Richard Koch

Chapter 7 Summary Questions

Optimal Training Principle #6: All behavior is caused. All causation is mental. We become what we think about most of the time.

How well we create a "mental representation" of the task often determines how well we can execute it. That includes how it feels to do it physically. Experts understand the activities so well that they are able to identify the right activity at the right time and execute it the right way. In order to create a strong mental representation we need to maintain a strong combination of passion and concentration. The book includes some simple strategies that can be used to create strong habits of thought. *We want athletes to understand that all behavior starts in our heads. As a result, we need to approach training with passion, focus, and a goal to continually improve our mental representations.*

Key Takeaways

1. All of your training activities should be considered to ensure they are effective and being executed efficiently. The goal is to consider them until we can do them without thinking about them.

2. The combination of passion and concentration determines how well we execute our behaviors. We should aim to pursue activities where we can maintain a high degree of both.

3. To create effective habits of behavior, we need to first create effective habits of thought.

- Actively considering your activities makes you inefficient. So why is it important to do it?
- How would you describe a "mental representation" in your own words?
- The Law of Conservation of Mental Energy says that "if you can do something without thinking, you will." Why is this the case?
- Why do we need to have both passion and concentration?
- What are some simple habits of thought that you can adopt?

Thought-provoking questions that may spark their interest/imagination.
- Why would a well-organized room or time spent away from your phone help your training?
- How often do you wake up in the morning knowing what your top few activities for the day need to be?
- On a scale of 1-10, how would you rate your passion and concentration in running?
- Could you create a very well-defined but BAD mental representation? How could that happen?
- Why is it so hard for many people to publicly state and commit to their goals?
- Have you ever found yourself doing something on "auto-pilot?" What are pros and cons of that experience?
- Passion + motivation = engagement; passion + concentration = purposeful training; what does motivation + concentration equal? (*Bryan's answer: quality execution.*)

Passion vs Concentration

		Degree of Focus	
		Distraction	Concentration
Degree of Interest	Passion	Mistakes	Purposeful
	Disinterest	Poor Behavior	Faking It

Team Activity - Passion vs Concentration

Think about what activities fall under each bucket of the Passion vs Concentration scale. You can use school, sports, hobbies, or anything that meets the below criteria. Where does this sport fit for you? If it's difficult to put it in one box, split it into multiple parts (practicing vs competing, etc). Compare to the answers your teammates came up with.

	Often Distracted	Easy to stay focused
Passionate		
Disinterested		

Takeaways

Write down any observations, strategies, or personal goals you want to make sure you remember.

"Watch your thoughts, they become words. Watch your words, they become actions. Watch your actions, they become habit." - Laozi

Chapter 8 Summary Questions

Optimal Training Principle #7: Optimal training is centered on clear, executable goals. We train to improve specific abilities.

There are two types of goals, North Star goals and Next Step goals. North Star goals motivate us to pursue a future result. Next Step goals determine how well we practice today. In order to develop a strong mental representation and get the most out of our training, we need to practice purposefully. This means improving specific abilities, focusing, getting immediate feedback, and stretching our limits. In terms of goal-setting it's more important how we choose and plan for a goal than what the goal actually is. *We want athletes to understand that goal-setting is not just setting North Star goals, but setting detailed Next Step goals that they can execute via purposeful practice in each workout.*

- What are the difference between North Star goals and Next Step goals?
- What are the four key components of Purposeful Practice?
- What are some ideas for making Naive practice time more purposeful?
- What does "goals are worthless but goal-setting is everything" mean?

Key Takeaways

1. There are two main types of goals, executional and motivational. Next Step goals are things we focus on in the moment. North Star goals are outcomes we hope to achieve in the future.

2. Purposeful practice is the key to maximizing your training. Clear execution goals are essential to purposeful practice, as are intense focus, immediate feedback and going outside our comfort zone.

3. North Star goals are primarily useful as drivers of motivation. We maximize their value when we align them with our core values, identify potential obstacles, and plan for all the ways we might not achieve them.

Thought-provoking questions that may spark their interest/imagination.
- Where do you see yourself in five years? What do you need to do in the next hour?
- Which of the four components of Purposeful Practice is most important? Why?
- How does purposeful practice develop better mental representations?
- Did any of the goal-setting strategies resonate with you? Which ones? Why?
- Why might failing be an important part of purposeful practice?
- How much of achieving a goal is identifying obstacles vs pushing hard to achieve it?

North Star vs Next Step Goals

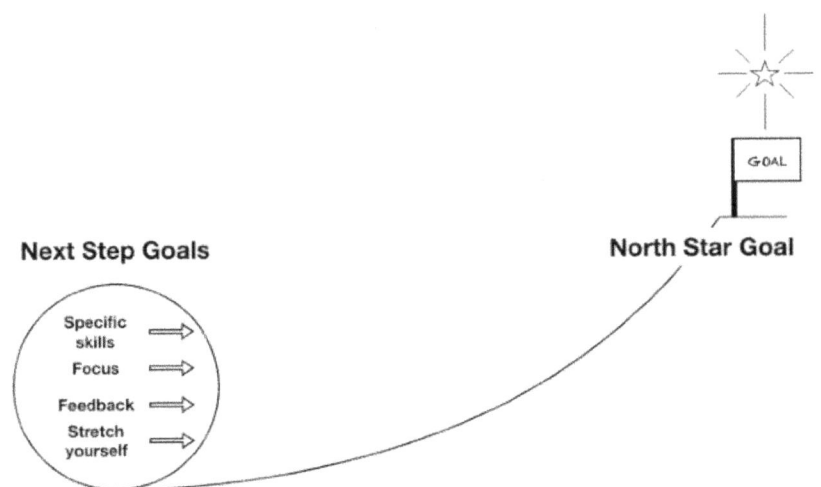

GOAL

North Star Goal

Next Step Goals

Specific skills ⟹

Focus ⟹

Feedback ⟹

Stretch yourself ⟹

Team Activity - Purposeful Practice

There are four components of Purposeful Practice. Think about your event and write down what a good example of each could be. Then, write down a strategy or idea to help you achieve it. Compare to the answers your teammates came up with.

	Example	Strategy to achieve it
Improve specific skills		
Intense focus		
Immediate feedback		
Get outside comfort zone		

Takeaways

Write down any observations, strategies, or personal goals you want to make sure you remember.

"Practice does not make perfect. Only perfect practice makes perfect." - Vince Lombardi

Next Level 80/20 Summary Questions

Next Level 80/20 is the act of applying 80/20 thinking to itself. When we have a lot of activities we could do, we can use Next Level 80/20 to find the "Most Effective" activity to focus on. Level 1 are the 20% activities: creating an optimal training mindset. Level 2 are the 4% activities: purposeful practice. Level 3 is the 1% activity: for runners, it is working hard day in and day out. Rest of 80% activities provide little value and just need to stay positive. We should put as much energy into each of these activities as we expect to gain from them. *We want athletes to critically think about where they invest their time, and to aim to identify and emphasize the most important activities.*

- What does it mean to apply the 80/20 Rule to itself?
- How would you explain the "Most Effective" activity to someone using the 80/20 Rule?
- Can you think of an example where just 4% of your effort generated 2/3 of your results?
- Can you think of an example where 2/3 of your effort generated just 4% of your results?
- For the "Rest-of-80%" why should you only worry about keeping them positive? Why not maximize those?

Next Level 80/20: 3 Insights

1. 80/20 thinking doesn't stop at Level 1. Once you've identified Level 1, you can use the 80/20 Rule on that group of activities, too.

2. There is one "Most Effective" activity. We can't put our energy into that activity unless we've taken the time to figure out what it is.

3. The "Most Effective" activity is enormously important. It may not account for 50% of our results, but it could. It will definitely have a 10x return compared to most other activities.

Thought-provoking questions to spark your athletes' interest/imagination.
- What are you doing today to ensure you can maximize your Level 3 activity tomorrow?
- Do you know the purpose for all your key workouts? Have you confirmed with your coach?
- Can 15 minutes of your day lead to 50% of your productivity? Explain.
- Do mistakes also follow the Next Level 80/20 rule?
- Can one person be the cause of 50% of your happiness or sadness?
- Using Next Level 80/20, how should you think about who you spend time with?
- How does Next Level 80/20 help us to think about our strengths and weaknesses?

80/20 Levels 2 and 3

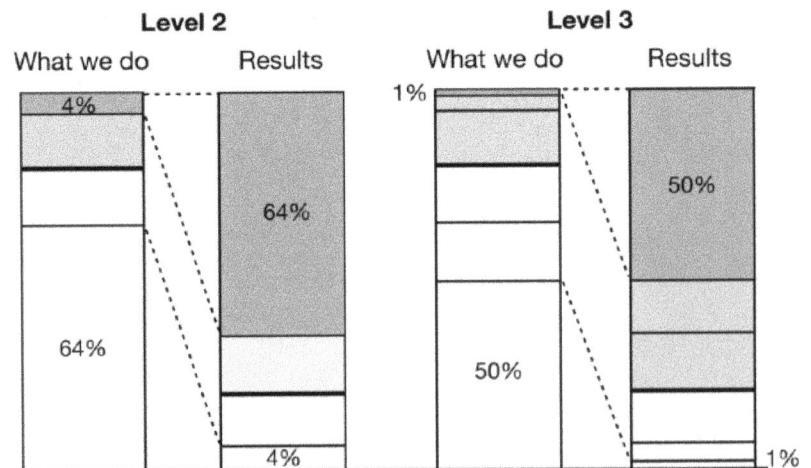

Team Activity - Next Level 80/20

Level 3 activities are the most important to maximize, followed by Level 2, Level 1, and Rest-of-80%. Pick an activity for each level and write down an idea to improve it in your training. Remember, Rest-of-80% activities should be minimized, not maximized...reduce effort. Compare to the answers your teammates came up with.

	Activity	Strategy to Improve it
Level 3 (top 1%)		
Level 2 (top 4%)		
Level 3 (top 20%)		
Rest-of 80%		

Takeaways

Write down any observations, strategies, or personal goals you want to make sure you remember.

"Time management is an oxymoron. Time is beyond our control, and the clock keeps ticking regardless of how we live our lives. Priority management is the key to maximizing the time we have."
- John C. Maxwell

Chapter 9 Summary Questions

Optimal Training Principle #8: Certain behaviors, if practiced with consistent quality, ensure Optimal Training.

Discipline in practice and in your lifestyle is fundamental to success. It's not maintained by willpower, however. It is maintained by optimizing your environment and routines, to create a positive "lazy default." This is best done by thinking in terms of systems: simple, improvable routines that lead to positive results. A good system is: not central to a goal but still important, has an identifiable minimum, can be tied to a rule, and can be tied to our environment. *We want athletes to put most of their energy into high value practice activities, and systematize other areas of their lives in ways that create positive outcomes with minimal effort.*

- What is the Discipline Illusion? Why do we struggle to see it clearly?
- What is more important for maintaining discipline: willpower or your environment?
- What is the benefit of a system?
- What are some areas of your life that can benefit from systems?

Key Takeaways

1. The Discipline Illusion causes undisciplined people to think discipline is restrictive and exhausting. In fact, discipline can lead to easier decision-making and less energy spent.

2. Discipline is not the product of willpower. It is the product of aligning our "lazy default" behaviors and removing environmental obstacles.

3. A system is a set of behaviors designed to keep your momentum moving forward with the minimal effort required.

4. Systems are best used for non-training activities that have a high probability of affecting our overall performance. These include sleep, diet, hydration and other day-to-day activities.

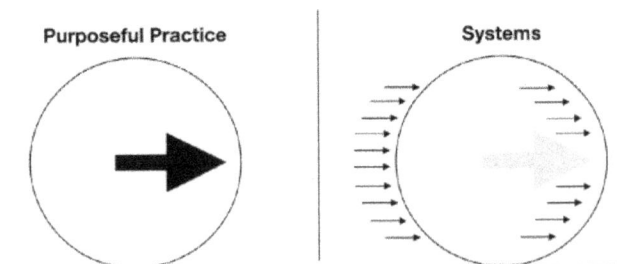

Thought-provoking questions that may spark their interest/imagination.
- Do you think sleep is a skill? How would you improve it if it were?
- What are some aspects of your environment that you have control over? What are some you don't control?
- True or False: some people have more willpower than others. True or False: those people are more successful.
- Do you have any effective systems you use today? What are they? Can they be improved?
- Do you have one area in particular that would benefit from a system? What is it?
- What is more likely to be successful, purposeful practice and poor systems, or naive practice and good systems?

Purposeful Practice vs Systems

Discipline Illusion

	Decisions	Restrictions	Willpower
Discipline Illusion	Too many	Too many No freedom No fun	Too much Exhausting
Actual Experience	Fewer Well-considered	Few Low priority items	Less Conserved for practice

Team Activity - Systems for Discipline

There are four questions to ask when creating a new system. Pick an area of your life to make a system, and then answer the questions. Compare to the answers your teammates came up with.

	A system for _____
How central is it to training?	*(Very = purposeful practice; Not very = system)*
What is the minimum?	
Can you make a rule?	
Can you optimize your environment?	

Takeaways

Write down any observations, strategies, or personal goals you want to make sure you remember.

"Even as you make progress, you need the discipline to keep from backtracking and sabotaging the success as it's happening." - Nipsey Hussle

Chapter 10 Summary Questions

Optimal Training Principle #9: Making mistakes is an effective way to learn and improve.

We need to embrace mistakes, but some mistakes are better than others. Mistakes of omission happen when we fail to act out of fear, stress, laziness, or distraction. We also can take the wrong action–mistakes of commission–due to ignorance or doing too much (striving). We cannot achieve a breakthrough performance unless we are willing to be bold and accept some risk. *We want athletes to push themselves and do work that leads to making a leap. That includes stretching their limits in practice and being bold in racing. They will make mistakes, but striving mistakes are a necessary risk.*

- What is the difference between a mistake of commission and a mistake of omission? Which is worse?
- What is a striving mistake? Can you give some examples of striving mistakes in training?
- What is the biggest negative to being overly Conservative?
- What is the difference between Bold and Reckless?

Thought-provoking questions that may spark their interest/imagination.
- What's the biggest training mistake you've ever made? What kind of mistake was it?
- What do you regret more: actions you took that ended up being mistakes, or actions you failed to take that ended up being mistakes?
- Could your team create a racing strategy that helped both conservative and reckless runners be more bold?
- In big races, many runners get conservative. Why? Is this good or bad?
- How does being more engaged in training help to limit mistakes?

Key Takeaways

1. A mistake of commission occurs because of your direct action. A mistake of omission occurs because you failed to take action. Both result from choices.

2. There are many types of mistakes, but the most valuable are Striving mistakes. These are mistakes you make because you are trying to do something new, pushing beyond your previous experiences.

3. Risk is an essential element of optimal training. It is best to approach your training with a Bold strategy that includes some risk along with a clear plan to achieve your goal.

Risk and Performance

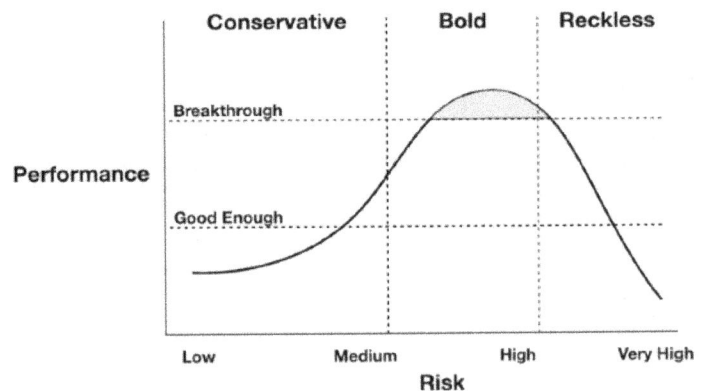

4 Types of Mistakes

	Ability to Correct	
	Easier	Harder
Omission	Laziness & Distraction	Fear & Stress
Commission	Ignorance	Striving

Team Activity - Mistakes

Write down examples of two mistakes you've made, one mistake of omission (when you failed to act) and one mistake of commission (where you did act). Thinking back on those experiences, what did you learn. Compare to the answers your teammates came up with.

	What happened?	What did you learn?
Omission (didn't act)		
Commission (did act)		

Takeaways

Write down any observations, strategies, or personal goals you want to make sure you remember.

"Take risks. Ask big questions. Don't be afraid to make mistakes. If you don't make mistakes, you aren't reaching far enough." - David Packard

Chapter 11 Summary Questions

Optimal Training Principle #10: Racing times and personal records indicate progress at one point in time.

Just as ability is variable, our performances only indicate progress at that point in time. Our performances do not indicate our talent or potential, and neither do other people's. When we receive criticism, we need to ensure it is constructive as it will not always come to us in a constructive format. How we think about our performances should be guiding us to improve our behaviors. *We want athletes to focus on effort and quality over time. We need to seek out feedback and criticism, but it needs to be effort-based if it is to be useful.*
  • What do your performances indicate about you? Does a good performance mean more than a bad performance?
  • Why is it so easy to associate other people's success with their talent?
  • What is the problem with receiving criticism from others? How can we make sure it is constructive?
  • What does "Respect your position while preparing for your promotion" mean to you?

Key Takeaways

1. It is important to not get fixated on your performances in the moment. They are only indications of where you are at a single point in time.

2. Be careful how you attribute the success of others. It is easy to fall into a fallacy of thinking others are succeeding because of their talent alone.

3. Translate criticism into effort-based terms. It will be easier to apply it constructively to your training.

4. The point of all your analysis is to prepare you to achieve your future goals. Develop excellent behaviors now to achieve excellent results in the future. Act as if.

Thought-provoking questions that may spark their interest/imagination.
  • You feel great after a good race and terrible after a bad race. Should you?
  • Do you wish people understood the context of your situation better? Do you make an effort to do that for others?
  • What are some simple guidelines you can use for giving criticism to others?
  • When someone beats you, it indicates a gap in your ability or preparedness. How does that gap change between competitions?
  • If you had enough time, how good could you be?

The Talent Trap

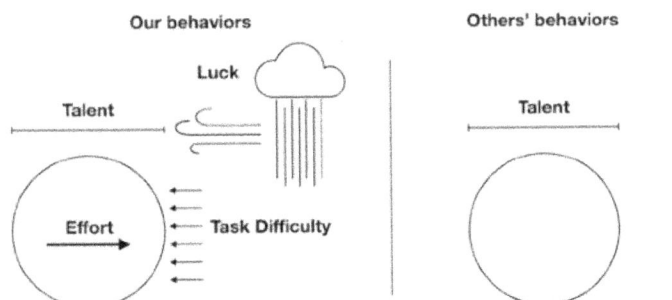

Different Abilities, Same You

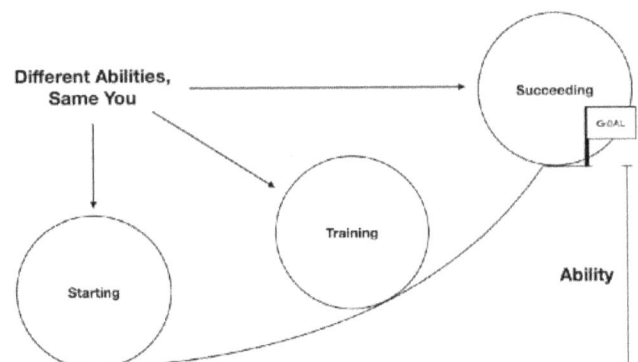

Team Activity - Criticism

Write down examples of a few times you've received criticism that <u>wasn't</u> effort-based. What happened and what advice or feedback did you receive? Now, how can you convert that feedback into effort-based terms that are more actionable? Compare to the answers your teammates came up with.

What happened?	Criticism you received	Convert it to effort

Takeaways

Write down any observations, strategies, or personal goals you want to make sure you remember.

"Not even analysis, by itself, can transform you. You must still do the changing yourself." - Natalie Wood

Chapter 12 Summary Questions

Optimal Training Principle #11: Optimal performances and realizing your potential are results of painstaking preparation and hard work.

Perseverance means to stick with something over time and despite obstacles. The more we can align our lives in positive ways, the easier this will be. In the short term, we focus on improving our largest arrows. Over the long term, we need to continually align all of our arrows to make them as positive as possible. This is often done via systems. One obstacle all runners deal with is injury. We should prepare the support we will need now to sustain momentum later. *We want athletes to appreciate that while there are no short-cuts to success, we can keep it simple and continually improve our situation. This makes persisting through adversity easier.*

- What do we need to focus on in the short-term? What are some examples?
- What do we need to focus on in the long-term? What are some examples?
- If injuries are inevitable, what's the best strategy to deal with them?
- Why is patience/persistence such an important aspect of achieving your potential?

Key Takeaways

1. Realizing your potential is the sum of many optimal performances over years and years of training. It doesn't come easily.

2. In the short-term, focus on the biggest factors: purposeful practice, consistent effort, good health, a strong relationship with your coach and mentor, and removing any major negative forces.

3. In the long-term, focus on aligning all the small forces in your life. The sum of these small forces is powerful. The best athletes keep every aspect of their lives as positive as possible.

4. Injuries are an inevitable part of training, and you need to prepare for them. Having a support network in place is critical for getting back on track.

Thought-provoking questions that may spark their interest/imagination.
- What is the biggest, most important factor driving your success today? Is it positive or negative? Internal or external? Is it a persistent force or a large obstacle?
- What would be the ideal training environment for you?
- Overtraining is a typical striving mistake. Can using the idea of the feedback loop or momentum model help to avoid over-training?
- Can you achieve your potential without a strong support network?

Today = Think Big

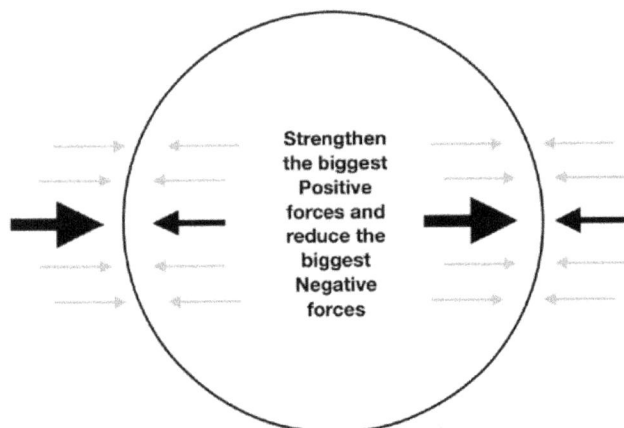

Strengthen the biggest Positive forces and reduce the biggest Negative forces

Tomorrow = Think Small, Think All

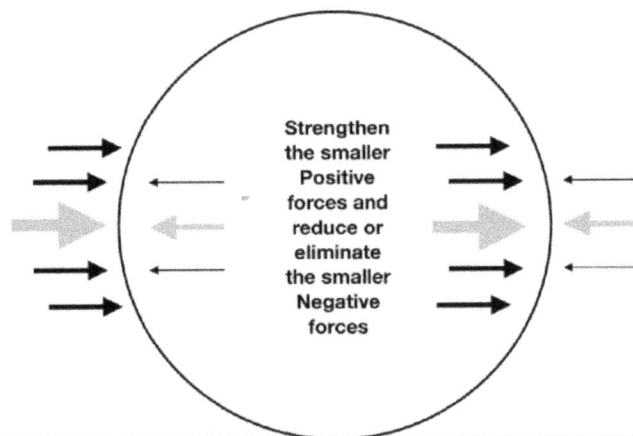

Strengthen the smaller Positive forces and reduce or eliminate the smaller Negative forces

Team Activity - Think Big

What are the biggest positive and negative forces affecting your momentum today? What are some ideas for improving the positive forces and reducing the negative forces? Compare to the answers your teammates came up with.

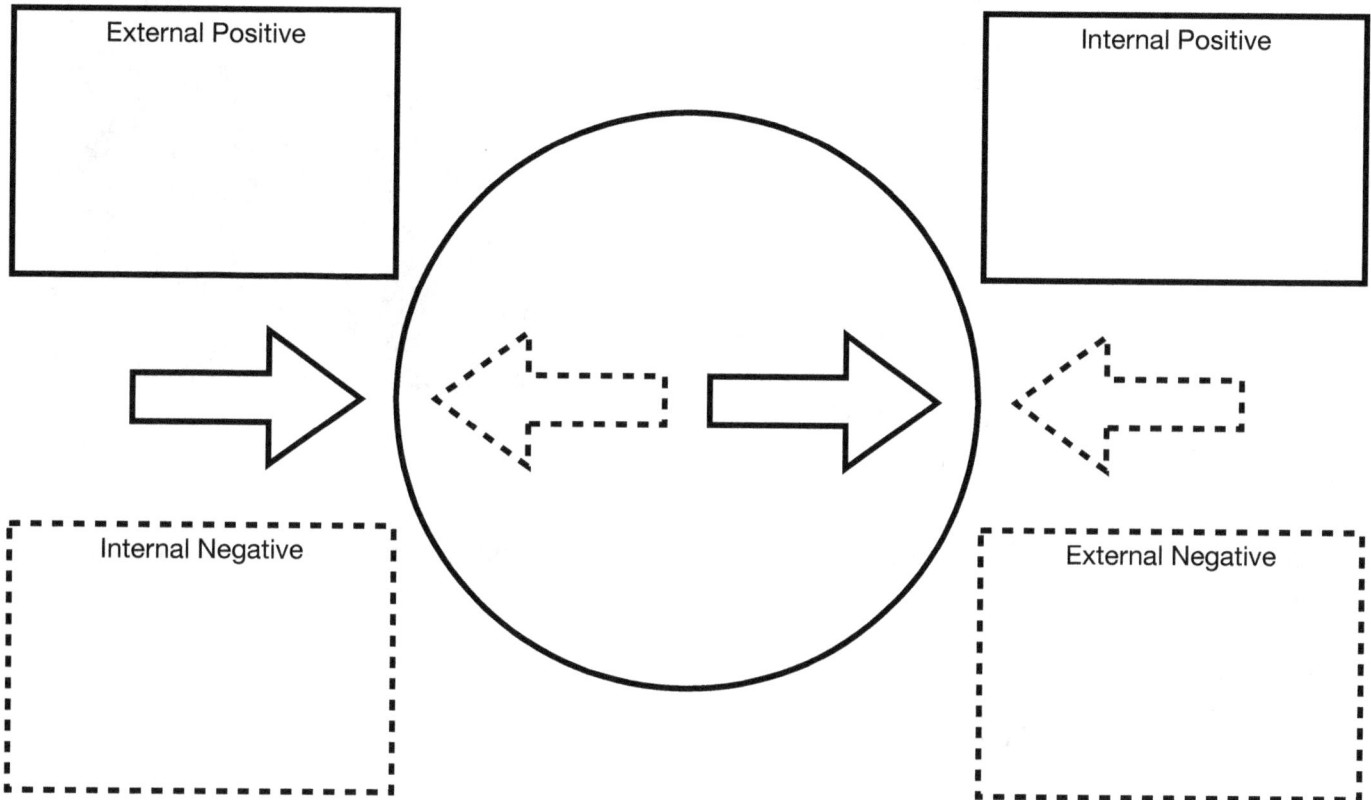

External Positive

Internal Positive

Internal Negative

External Negative

Takeaways

Write down any observations, strategies, or personal goals you want to make sure you remember.

"Focusing on the right priorities can help you do more faster." - David Cohen

About Bryan Green

Bryan Green is the author of Make the Leap, co-founder of Go Be More apparel, and co-host of the Go Be More Podcast and Fueling the Pursuit Podcast. He lives in Sendai, Japan with his wife and two daughters. Prior to moving to Japan he used the same mindset in this book to excel in his career at Apple and to learn Japanese and Italian as an adult.

He competed at UCLA from 1997 to 2002, and was a two-time individual qualifier to the NCAA Cross Country Championships in 2000 and 2001.

HS bests (3rd best time*)
800m: 1:59 (2:00)
1600m: 4:23 (4:26)
3200m: 9:22 (9:29)
XC (3mi): 15:17 (15:35)

Collegiate bests
1500m: 3:50.1 (3:52)
5000m: 14:19 (14:22)
10000m: 29:25 (29:40)
XC (8k): 23:57 (24:11)

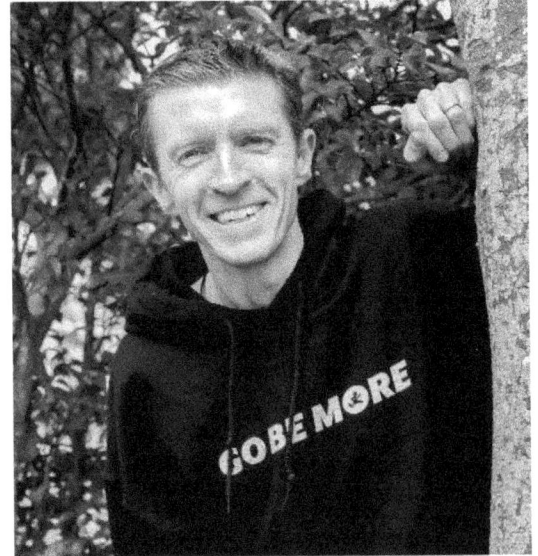

* My teammate Scott Abbott used to argue that one's 3rd best time is a more accurate reflection of their actual ability. I agree.

Make the Leap
A simple, practical framework to think better, train better, and run faster.
Email: bryan@maketheleapbook.com
Website: maketheleapbook.com
Social: @maketheleapbook

Go Be More
Clothing to boost commitment: your clothes should inspire you to be more.
Website: gobemore.co
Social: @gobemoreapparel

Podcasts
Interviews with Olympians, elite athletes, performers and high achievers exploring how they do what they do.
Go Be More Podcast: gobemore.co/gobemorepodcast
Fueling the Pursuit Podcast: ucan.co/podcast

Get my Think Better Newsletter!

I expand on the topics in Make the Leap and offer simple tips to think better about training and life. It's one idea, one system, and one question...in one email per week.

Sign up at maketheleapbook.com/newsletter.

www.ingramcontent.com/pod-product-compliance
Lightning Source LLC
Chambersburg PA
CBHW080939040426

42443CB00015B/3474